MW01264937

Table of Contents

Introduction

What's the greatest misconception about Trade Show Marketing?

Is it that everyone is making a killing at shows and you are not?

Is it that you should have built-in trade show selling skills and great results should be easy?

Is it that you can't stop attending a show because "what will people say?"

The truth is that trade show marketing and selling is a series of skills that, like any skill can be developed and focused to produce exceptional results *for any company.*

Many companies spend large portions of their marketing budgets on trade shows, and the industry isn't showing any signs of going away any time soon.

So really, the question is: What role can trade shows play in helping you meet your overall marketing and business objectives?

Know the answer to that question and you are ahead of 90% of exhibitors.

This Guide is designed to focus your efforts step by step so that you put your resources into getting the best return on your marketing money that you can.

What the world needs is not more trade show marketing information but *precise* trade show marketing information.

If you follow the steps in this book – *and apply them to your trade show marketing efforts* – you will get better results.

And these days, who doesn't want more leads and more deals closed from those leads?

Mitch Tarr
Lake Havasu City, AZ

Planning the Show Strategy

This is where most trade shows marketing campaigns are won or lost--effective planning.

There are 101 items to look after, decisions to be made, things to produce, people to train, suppliers to work with and never enough time in the day.

Trade shows are one of the most complicated types of marketing.

But many people, especially first-timers look for the easy way out. "Just tell me what to do." they say. But it's not as simple as that.

Everything to do with the show is related to something else in the show. Increase this, decrease that, focus on this, and minimize that. How do you really know which is which?

My favourite example of how this can go
wrong is a show we attended in Las Vegas
in 2002. We had a team of 3 working on
show preparation.

We needed to produce a new shirt for our
uniform. Seemed simple enough.

Then it started. The project lead for the
show couldn't let the person assigned to
the task complete the task. Between the
two of them they killed hours in a territory
dispute over when the shirts were to be
done, what supplier to use, and the style to
select.

On top of that, everyone wanted a hand in
selecting the style. Some liked this, some
liked that, and some wanted the cheapest.

We literally wasted hours on these shirts.
We had yelling, running to managers, the
CEO throwing in his two cents. It was a
mess.

Why did it go like that?

Well the simple thing was I didn't set out the ground rules for what was important. I didn't train my staff that this line item was only one piece in the puzzle. If you are building a 500-piece jigsaw puzzle, why spend more time on any single piece than you should? What would be the effect of getting this completely wrong?

How would it affect our goals?

It was a great lesson in show management. Even though we had a great checklist and project plan, accountabilities and deadlines, we were spinning our wheels.

So the moral of this story and the purpose of this book are to help you focus on the key items that will get you the best results for the least amount of money.

Good Exhibiting.

Review Previous Show Goals and Results

When was the last time you held a quick meeting to ask the specific question? "How did we do at our last show?"

Did we hit our targets? What went well? What was a problem? What did we learn? Knowing what you know now, would you return? Now that you have been to the show does the show still fit with your marketing strategy and plans?

Hold a quick meeting and do a review.

Team Debriefing

One of the most common questions I hear is which shows should we be in?

Like someone else could instantly know which show fits your goals and which wouldn't. One way to find shows to attend is to use a resource that is sitting right under your nose.

Gather the staff together for a short debriefing meeting on past shows. Many people working for you attended shows when they worked for someone else in your industry.

Simply ask what shows they went to in the past and what can they tell you about it?

Ask your staff the question.

Hit the World Wide Web

Your competitors are great. Why? Because they will often post on their websites the shows they are going to attend and exhibit at.

Do some research and see if there are any patterns. Are they all at one show? Or are they spread over many different shows?

Keep in mind that your goal is not to follow the crowd but to compile a list of possible shows to exhibit at.

Once you have a list to select from you can start to narrow it down. But the first step is to build the list.

Compile a list of possible shows.

Call a Customer

Contact your ideal and best customers and ask them what shows they attend to stay abreast of the industry and make buying decisions.

They may surprise you by identifying a regional conference or an industry trade show you weren't aware of.

Customers often notice that you take the time to be in step with them. You may just have earned a few respect points by making the call.

It's possible you will know more about the shows to attend than they do, and suddenly they are asking for your advice!

Everything you can do to differentiate yourself can and will make a difference.

Ask your customers to help with your list.

Review the Big Picture

Review your big picture sales and marketing goals and plans. Make sure you can identify what role your trade show will play in your overall marketing plans.

Be specific. For example:

Our goal this year is to expand sales by 20%. We will do this by increasing the leads fed to the sales force through direct mail, trade shows and the Internet.

We plan to hold our marketing budget flat.

Now you go the show planning session with this question in context. How can your trade show get more leads? Do we need more shows? Better lead generation? Different shows?

Each show should have its own goals and should be in sync with your corporate goals.

As a small company you may be saying, sure I'll just hold a meeting with myself and see if the show will help me.

But what actually happens in real life is an event salesman calls and invites you to exhibit and the show is fast approaching so you don't have time to do your homework.

Or your local Chamber of Commerce is holding a show and your networking peers are checking to see if you are going.

Resist the temptation to go with the flow. Just because one show works for one company, don't assume it will work for you.

Hold the meeting to set the specific show objectives.

Plan Your Year's Announcements

One of the best reasons to attend a trade show is to make a product announcement.

You have customers there. You have prospects there. You have strangers (who may be qualified prospects there). Your business partners and key suppliers may be there. You have media and analysts there. (This is BIG)

And, if you are good you have your competitors there (and they are unprepared for your announcement!)

Shows are great places to make product announcements. Every year at the CES in Las Vegas Bill Gates used to make big announcements in his keynote speech and the whole world focused on it.

Don't you think that his organization is working from the show date backward in their planning?

If you plan to attend multiple shows make sure you make a list of planned company milestones and announcements such as product launch, merger/acquisition, market research, pricing action and partner announcements.

Which ones match a show date?

Set your timeline and work from the trade show backwards.

List Your Specific Measurable Goals

Goals seem easy. You think everyone has them. I always ask clients the question. "What are your key show goals?"

It never fails to amaze me that marketing teams don't have them.

Even worse, if I ask the same question of the 10 people flying in from around the country to participate in the show, they don't know either.

How would you expect them to maximize this marketing opportunity when they don't know what a successful outcome is?

Develop specific expected trade show results. State how you know you will have achieved your show results. It could read. "We expect 55 **qualified** sales leads from this show" or "We expect 12 media interviews" or "We expect to meet 10 new Executives in our industry."

Be specific. Write them down. Send them out to the team.

Identify Your Market Segment

Why are smaller regional shows making progress over the giant international all-industry shows?

Often it's because the show management knows their audience. They know how to segment them.

Try this exercise to ID your audience.

Where are they from? (Geographic)

What is their profession? (Trade)

What is their job title? (VP Sales, CEO, Network Admin)

How big a company do they work for?

Identify and document Key Market Segments (geographic, industry, job title)

Make sure they match yours.

Search Out All Possible Shows

Make a list of all possible shows, conferences, and events that could be related to your show goals.

Take all of your research from all the sources we talked about and make a list of the shows.

The first time I did this for my industry I thought, "What good will this be? I know all the shows."

BUT

When I made the list and put down the dates, suddenly a plan took form.

We could organize our efforts around times and locations and other events. (Remember your product launch timeline?)

Then when we talked about our show plan, we knew we had to make choices. Our budget didn't allow us to go to every show.

So we made the following adjustments.

One: we moved a product announcement date forward to capitalize on a critical show.

Two: we split one big show into two smaller ones to have a steady stream of leads to feed the sales force with.

Three: we cancelled an unrelated show.

Four: we walked the floor of a local show to evaluate it for next year.

All from a list that I didn't think would help all that much!

Make your list.

Brainstorm Different Marketing Campaigns

It's not uncommon for marketing departments to take the same old booth, same old staff, same old brochures, same old draw, and same old giveaway, and do it again.

It is a great idea to stop and consider the following question.

"What can I do for this show that will help ensure we make our Show Objective?

Then ask yourself this question…

"What can I do for this show that **is completely unique** and will ensure we make our Show Objective?

Brainstorm unique and different marketing campaigns. Don't get too attached to one show strategy. Attempt to look at all the possible ways to meet your show objectives.

Then make changes. Don't fall into the trap of repeating what you did last year—just because.

Things change.

Hold a trade show brainstorming meeting with the right team members.

Add up the Numbers

Calculate total trade show costs. Make a budget for your show. Take a look for more effective or efficient ways to attend.

Seems simple. Right?

Of course you counted the freight. And the duty for shipping to France? And all the staff you have planned? The new graphics? The special giveaways? The surcharges for missing some deadlines?

You get my point.

You will have lots of room to see a $10,000 show budget turn into more. I saw an article recently, which suggested you keep 4% of your budget as a guideline for travel.

I know I can't get two people to New York and back for that.

Be realistic. Pretend you will miss some deadlines and pay the higher rate.

Imagine you will need something you didn't plan for. You'll think of something if you spend the time.

As you run more shows you will learn to count all the items and be a better forecaster.

Wouldn't it be better to report your $10,000 show cost you $10,000? It's much better than having to try to understand why $10,000 became $14,000!

Do a line by line budget.

Calculate your Show ROI

This important calculation is designed to give you a benchmark Return on Investment (ROI) for your trade show.

The calculation is very simple.

Take your show goals. E.g. Generate 100 NEW leads.

Then take your show budget. $7,500.00

Now divide the two.

$7,500.00/100 leads = $75.00 per lead.

In this case each lead cost you $75.00.

How does that compare to other shows or other means of generating leads?

With these numbers you can decide if the show is just too expensive or a great bargain.

For small business owners, don't forget the value of your time. Include setting up and breaking down the show.

Calculate the ROI for every show, every year.

Get Help from Business Partners, Alliances or Key Suppliers

List possible partner resources that could be shared.

You work with suppliers or partners or resellers in the field all year long.

Can your business partner send a person to demonstrate your product also? Can a client show how they use your product?

Does your business partner have co-op funding to support your exhibiting in a show to sell their products?

Are they going to a show and can you participate in their booth?

I have a client that attends the large industry show every year, and never buys a booth. They take a table in one of their key supplier's booths.

They call customers and prospects by phone in advance of the show and set up face-to-face meetings. They save a fortune.

Explore possible sources of co-funding.

Write a Show Objective Statement

Keep a written show objective statement handy for your show. Share it with staff and partners and vendors so everyone is on the same page and can support your efforts.

During the show planning stages and the pre-show execution stage, new ideas are then presented against a better show result instead of randomly.

It's much easier to ask people how this will further the show objectives of acquiring 55 qualified leads instead of debating color preferences for a shirt selection.

Or during the staff training pre-show you now have a tool to keep people focused.

During the show itself you have something to point to during the breakfast meetings to reinforce your goals.

Write and publish your show goals.

One Person Only-One Person Only

Make one person responsible and accountable for show results.

This maxim is true for shows as in any other endeavour.

Lots of items have to be done on time for a show to happen successfully.

If one person owns the list, checks up on the list, revises the list, reports on the list, you have less of the old, "I though Sally was looking after that" omissions.

Assign a show manager.

All Data in One Place

Create a trade show binder.

Keep a physical copy of all work orders, contracts, input forms, waybills, agreements, schedules, training information, travel info, meeting times, schedules, and checklists.

Keep one for each show. There will be lots of opportunity for people to ask questions.

Did we ship this item? How many brochures are arriving? Where are we

staying? What does the electrical cost?
(This one comes from the CFO all the time!)

The point is that if one person is managing
the project and all the material is in one
place then EVERYONE else knows where
to go to get answers.

Create a show binder.

Create a Show Playbook

Unlike the show binder, this is the tool that
you give to each of your staff that exhibits
at the show.

You should include some of the following
sections to ensure everyone knows what to
expect.

1. Show Goal Statement
2. List specific measurable results
3. Locations and Maps (convention
   center, hotels, event locations)
4. Cell phone numbers of the team
5. Set up and breakdown time
6. List of responsibilities in the city

7. Booth schedule
8. How the draw works
9. How to qualify prospects
10. Expected follow up plan

Remember to ensure that everyone knows
that this is a confidential document.

When the show is over, make sure
everyone knows to return his or her copy.

Copies out = copies in.

***Make and distribute a trade show
playbook.***

Read and Know the Show Rules

Review the rules. Know what the event
managers expect from you in terms of
conduct, setup and breakdown times and
logistics.

At one point you will be standing there
ready to open your booth and you will be
asking yourself a question like. "I was sure
I was allowed to have a live goldfish in the
booth."

You're in a strange city – Cleveland for example (just kidding) and you don't have a back up plan.

How easy would it have been to review the show rules, which state categorically that there are no live fish allowed on the show floor?

Every show is different just like each convention center is different and each has its own rules.

Ignore them at your peril.

Read and review the rules AND keep a copy in your show binder.

Do Reconnaissance

Have someone on board who knows the city you are going into. Local knowledge can help you find restaurants for clients, convenient hotels, and shortcuts.

We were attending a show in Las Vegas and met a Japanese delegation on the Monday.

We agreed to host them for dinner the following night. Our choices would have been limited if we had to rely on second hand information about restaurants.

Fortunately I knew of a Sushi restaurant that would meet our needs for quiet space and good food.

They were impressed that we knew about a restaurant that was so good. It was a small thing but it made a difference.

Ensure you have some local knowledge so you can add some value to your client meetings or simply know that catching a cab cross town in the rain in Manhattan is a challenging thing to do.

Find your local knowledge source in case you need it.

Call the Event Manager

One area that is often overlooked is the relationship with the event manager.

Many exhibitors feel like they can treat the event manager with little or no respect and still get top-notch service, prime booth location, and even exceptions to the show rules.

In case you don't know it, the event manager's job is a challenging one.

Balancing the needs of exhibitors, delegates, vendors, facilities and timelines is a harrowing job.

Show some empathy, build your relationship, think long term, and you will be able to have greater and greater success in a particular show.

Contact the event manager immediately when you decide to participate in a show and build your relationship with them.

A cooperative strong partnership with an event manager will be more likely to get exceptions, perks, and special offers than a curt confrontational style.

Event managers are people too.

Find Your Travel Expert

Have someone on board who knows travel.

If you have ever had to fly through Chicago in the snow, Dallas in a spring thunder shower, or New York any time, you will know that weather can affect your ability to host an exhibit.

First, plan some time in your schedule to allow for missed connections and lost luggage.

Then make sure you know the location of the hotel, conference center, and airport relative to each other.

Will you need a car? What are you planning to carry in your carry on? Are you bringing key booth material with you or shipping everything?

Where are connections going to be tight, and where do you have some space.

What happens when your setup team shows up at the airport at 6 am Sunday to fly from Seattle to Houston only to discover they didn't allow enough time to clear security? They're no good to you at the airport in the wrong city!

Ignore your travel expert at your own risk.

Book Your Travel – NOW!

One thing you will most certainly discover is how much it costs to fly 10 people across the country on short notice.

Or as has happened to us, you go to book one of the block of rooms at the hotel at the conference rate only to discover the conference rate rooms are long gone.

One thing we used to do was check a Priceline.com booking for the show dates as soon as we confirmed we would attend. More than once we were able to beat the conference price simply by trying. In a non-sold out situation, that worked for us.

Earlier, better planning for your T&C expenses can certainly allow you to attend at a lower cost and therefore to improve your ROI.

Try a bit harder to contain your T&C expenses.

Your CFO will love you.

Hire Professional Booth Staff

Consider hiring show staff in the city you are attending the show. Travel costs will be nil and you can get some very professional help to work the booth.

Just because someone doesn't work in your employ, doesn't mean they can't learn your qualifying question, your USSP and how to generate leads for you.

There are companies that make their entire business to supply staff for shows.

Before you assume I am talking about hiring models (male or female) for their looks, remember your show goal.

Getting people to your booth and being unable to qualify them is the same as not getting people in your booth.

So ask yourself the question, what type of staff could complement my show strategy and meet my goal of **"insert show goal here."**

Don't underestimate the value of magicians, hawkers, actors, celebrities, dancers, etc to draw a crowd.

Do a Booth ROI Calculation Each Year

Review booth size and costing – renting vs. buying. Do a review every year to ensure your booth continues to meet your needs.

Is it modular? Will it grow with you? Can it be adapted to multiple show uses?

By spending the time to review this once a year (or more often) you will have the planning horizon to do a better job (and maybe a more cost effective job) for your shows.

> 1: Review your booth cost relative to your overall budget. Maintain a balance.

> 2: Keep in step with what your customers expect.

3: Keep it in line with your competitive positioning.

4: Review your show ROI and keep your booth cost relative.

5: Plan for more wear and tear on high-travel or high-maintenance booths.

6: Quality never goes out of style.

7: Consider upgrading your booth to a planned schedule.

The most important thing to remember is that the booth is just one component of an overall show strategy. Too much or too little won't work for you.

Conversely, a top of the line booth won't save you being in the wrong show with the wrong message!

Be Ruthless on Your Giveaway Budget

It's almost a certainty that 80% of booths will have something to give prospects, which causes them to stop.

I don't know where this tactic started but the pressure to fit in to the pack can be enormous.

The important task here is to consider what role your giveaway will play in meeting your show plan and goals and how people will react to it?

Back in the office, before the show, some real territory battles can take place. The issue of what to give away can be the center piece of meeting after meeting and there is risk of letting this line item skew your plan.

Calculate the cost of your giveaway. How much of your overall show budget is it? If it is 50% of your hard cost, is it 50% of the impact of your exhibit?

Review this one carefully. A pen with your logo on it in the hands of an unqualified prospect is a pen in the hands of a stranger on the street.

Here are some pointers to get the most mileage from the trade show promotional item.

1. Determine how this item will support your show goal.
2. Will you give it freely to all or will it help you qualify people?
3. Do the prospects have to earn it?
4. How will you answer the question: "Can I have 3? I have three kids?"
5. Make sure your item lands on the prospects desk.
6. Always aim for top quality.
7. Consider the fun factor.
8. Are they easy to transport?
9. Can they be used after the show?
10. Can you do without it?

Simply spend the time to evaluate how much this giveaway will support your goals. Remember it is only one piece of the trade show puzzle.

*Calculate the ROI on your giveaway.
Make it support your show goal, not the
other way around.*

What is Your Dress Code?

Ensure you have a booth uniform. It can
be from the simple blue shirt and tan pants
level up to a set of custom shirts with
custom logos. Everyone should be part of
the 'show brand.'

One of the best show brands I saw was at a
technology show in the middle of the dot
com era.

The company was McAfee and the product
was anti-virus software. In an exhibit hall
with hundreds of competitors, they were
dressed as doctors and nurses. Their
corporate colors were white and red. Their
booth was **memorable**.

You may not have to go to that extreme but
you do want to avoid your staff showing
up in the same clothes they would wear to
the office.

The typical solution is to have a golf shirt or polo shirt made with the logo on it. The people are as much a part of the booth brand as the signage is. Make sure they belong.

As an added benefit, you may take advantage of a great company name, product name, USP, or URL and have it embroidered across the back or down the arm of the shirt.

That way the billboard stands out as it moves around the show floor. Every little bit helps.

Make Uniform Selection a Small Line Item

Don't spend more than 2 hours on the show uniform.

Often the selection of a shirt style, colour, logo, sizes, quantities, and who is entitled can consume way more time and energy than it is worth in the big picture.

Use Your Executive Team

If you are bringing top management to the show make sure you invite your best client's top management to drop by for an introduction.

Upper management loves trade shows because it gives them a chance to be in the street with clients and prospects, check out competition, and do some team building.

Use this opportunity to move your contact levels higher up the organization.

That means spending some effort before the show to find out from your clients which of their executive team will be attending the show.

Make an effort to set a meeting between the two. You have lots of reasons to do so.

1. First look at new products
2. Reward excellent clients for past business. Dinner is great.
3. Probe for feedback on products or service levels

4. Introduce your client executive to someone you know that could help them
5. Quickly touch base to evaluate current industry trends.
6. Plan a round of golf pre or post show (always a winner!)

Your clients are paying to fly to the same location you are in.

They have their own reasons for attending, however you can work at attempting to help them with their goals and have a chance to make a new, long term relationship with a key client executive.

Set up executive-to-executive meetings <u>before</u> the show starts.

Hold Down the Fort

What is your coverage plan for back in the office during shows? Make sure you can handle leads, qualify opportunities and solve service issues.

If your sales reps are at the show make sure their clients know whom to call to get answers while you are gone.

Avoid the pitfall of having your sales staff think that the show is a vacation. It's plain old hard work.

Still, the job to be done back at the office is just as important.

Have a solid coverage plan for when your sales staff is at the show.

Logistics Needs a Detail Person

Put a detail person in charge of the checklist.

Really what you need here is a project manager. Get someone who knows how to make a timeline, assign responsibilities, delegate, follow up, monitor status, and adapt to issues.

If you look at each show as a project and have a team to work with you might consider having a different person for each show.

You will build some bench strength and have some back up in place in the unlikely event your key detail project manager goes away.

Go Introduce Yourself at the Show

Expand your relationship with show manager/show rep at the show.

Go see him or her when you get to the city.

Build this relationship. Yes, they are busy. You are too. But, when there is a chance to work outside the box, show managers will be more likely to do so if they know you.

Write a Checklist

Create a checklist with show milestones in it.

Brush up on your Microsoft Project skills. It isn't overkill to have a living breathing documented plan handy.

You can use this to walk through pre show meetings or simply to send out to remind people they are on a deadline.

Keeping everyone on the timeline is much easier.

You will also be less likely to miss an ordering deadline, which will end up costing you more money.

Ordering many show items are time sensitive and it is pretty easy to miss an order date to earn the discount.

There is no secret show plan that allows you to pay what you want **when** you want for show services.

Miss the cut off and you pay the premium.

You could even show up at the exhibit hall and head to the order desk only to find long lines of other good planners ordering their electrical, lighting, carpet upgrades too. I've seen this one a bit too often in my time.

Work from a show plan or checklist.

Pre Show Selling – Invitations (critical item)

The ability to use the time before a show to start the selling process is very often overlooked and the opportunity cost is huge.

Consider these two approaches.

One: Order 500 pairs of cheap sunglasses and give them out to anyone who walks by your booth, thus creating goodwill.

Two: Send an invitation to each of the 49 key executives in the companies on your targeted list. Invite them to pick up a pair of $140 Oakley sunglasses in your booth.

OK, now choose: ☐ One   ☐ Two

My choice would be two. (Let's assume our show goal is to meet new prospects)

Don't be surprised to find the 85% of the people you target make a point to come and visit your booth for a $140 pair of Oakley glasses. Wouldn't you?

Same show, same budget, same staff but different results!

Spend some time to invent a reason for prospects or clients (depending on your show goals) to attend your booth.

Bribe key prospects to visit your booth

Use Show Passes

Many event managers supply free passes for you to invite your customers and prospects to attend the show.

Spend a minute and decide if your show objective could be met by supplying passes to your best prospects, or oldest clients, or key suppliers.

If the answer is yes, call the event manger and ask if you can have double your allotment. Often they are happy to supply them.

Send a nice letter inviting everyone who wants a pass to pick one up. Or send the pass in the letter and let them forward to the right person.

But don't send an email and say a pass is available if you want one.

Build a preshow direct mail campaign.

What is Your Qualifying Question?

If you are attending trade shows to generate new leads you will want to, as closely as possible, follow your selling process.

The fact that you are at a show and everyone is giving away yo-yos shouldn't keep you from doing what you do in real sales situations—qualify your prospect.

I had a client who sold to small business owners.

Which of the following opening statements would have the best effect for him?

A: Hi, would you like to see my product?

B: Would you like a yo-yo?

C: Do you own a small business?

If you picked C (I surely hope you did) you are on your way to leveraging your trade show investment.

It is critical to know if you are talking to the people your marketing efforts are targeting. Just because someone is at a show doesn't mean they are your target audience.

They could be media (yay), competition (groan), or tire kickers (yikes).

Your success will be greater if you plan to qualify in the booth. Qualified prospects are like gold, you need to dig a little bit.

Remember to train your staff (all of them) to ask the sales question, "Are you my market?"

One of the single most important skills is to qualify whom you are talking to. Qualify with a professional business card exchange. Or ask them what they do. Or ask if they *insert opening line here.*

Always, always, always ask if they are your market.

Have a Show-specific USP

Sameness is the bane of all marketing. As you know, the Unique Selling Proposition is one way to start making sure people know you are different.

Make sure you also have a Unique Show Selling Proposition (USSP). It should look something like this.

"We are the biggest, oldest, best, fastest growing, (insert your business here)."

"We are the only company to provide over 77 different styles of widgets."

"We are the first company to ever deliver something like this."

Having a USSP is good. Training all of your show staff to know it is better and training them to use it is best of all.

Write and use a USSP.

Make Your Giveaway Sell

Trade show promotional items are a big part of the trade show universe.

Generally this is another one of those areas that plays a distorted role in helping you to achieve your overall goals.

By that, I mean many hours and meetings, and gnashing of teeth is spent over what would be the best giveaway for a show?

Here is where emotion, politics, and short-term thinking can hinder your show effectiveness.

Management gets involved and personal preferences takes priority over what gets the best result.

As you know, there are at least 10,000 things that can have your logo imprinted on them. So pick something that really supports your show goal.

What role does your show takeaway play in moving someone along the sales process?

Make sure you can identify its role. If the role is minimal or non-existent, consider not using them.

Make Your Marketing Material Sell

Same question, different area.

What role does your marketing material play in the sales process?

If you have a $4 brochure and want to give it to everyone passing your booth you may be falling into the trap of using existing marcom simply because you have lots of it on hand.

A large company brochure will surely end up in the same recycle bin as the other 100 heavy, glossy, expensive brochures your prospect has collected.

You may consider printing a postcard with a special show offer on it instead and making sure this gets in the hands of your target.

A short, targeted, sales copy driven marketing piece can really reinforce your show goals more effectively than the big expensive brochure and tie in nicely to the follow up action.

If you are launching a product, generating leads, garnering media attention or taking pricing action use a short dedicated sales piece.

Make your sales offer have some value and your sheet will have a better chance to escape the fate of the recycle bin.

The use of a short single purpose sales sheet or page, also has the benefit of saving you money, since you are giving away something that cost $.75 per item instead of $4.00.

Create a single sales copy driven handout to support your show objective.

Booth Design – Write a Headline!

What is the goal of your booth? Will it sell something for you? Will it qualify a prospect? Will it make a key alliance? Not on its own it won't. Your booth doesn't sell, people sell.

Yet people spend time and money on the booth like it will outperform the people in it.

In my opinion the role of the booth is twofold.

One. It should match your brand and leave a favourable impression of the brand promise.

Two. It should stop people in their tracks so they have to learn more about you.

How to do that?

One overlooked way is to use headlines in the same way that direct marketers have been doing for years.

The goal of a headline is to stop the reader long enough for them to consider that maybe, just maybe you have something that is of benefit to them.

And that my friend is when you hand off from the booth design to the trade show staff.

The booth has done its job. It has delivered to you a potential prospect. And they are self-qualified.

They stopped because your headline was of interest to them.

Use a headline with a key benefit in your booth graphics.

How to Write a Powerful Booth Headline

Remember the goal of a headline is to stop someone in their tracks and make them want to learn more.

So DO NOT

- be clever,

- be tricky,

- use a double meaning,

- be uninteresting,

- or self serving.

Instead DO

- offer your top benefit to the reader,

- be specific,

- be clear and concise.

Make the headline visible. Change it from
show to show to match your goals.

Just as good direct marketing copywriters
know the headline can make or break a
campaign so too can a good headline help
or hinder your show goals.

*Use good copywriting skills from your
direct response-driven marketing cousins.*

Planning the Show Details

Each show is different and once you have
the big picture plans and the key elements
in place, you simply need to make sure the
small items are looked after.

It's way better (trust me on this one) to be
ready for some of these little items up front
and not have to scramble when you get to a
show.

Get a Trade Show Swiss Army Knife

Bring a survival kit with the booth. That means duct tape, paper, Velcro, pens, phone numbers, spare parts, light bulbs, fasteners, holders, and anything that can be used to solve a last minute breakage problem.

Bring a small office worth of supplies.

Generally you will find that on set up day things don't quite go as planned. Small things break, last minute items crop up and you will be in a convention center far from Staples.

Make sure you also map out where the closest Staples is, so you can cab over there on Sunday afternoon and find the missing "insert last minute forgotten item here."

Fishing tackle boxes and toolboxes make good carrying cases for your Trade Show Swiss Army Knife items.

Plan for small annoying missing items and bring a supply with you.

Print Out Booth Setup Instructions

Booth setup is not a natural skill that is imprinted in everyone's DNA. Since you may only be setting a booth up 2 or 5 times a year the sequence of what steps go in what order can be open to interpretation.

Print out and bring booth setup and breakdown repacking directions. Many booth setups are self-evident but you would be surprised how many booths have small quirks that you find when you are already on the road.

Good booth companies keep copies online for your booth model.

Insert your printed instructions in your binder and in the booth crate.

Turn On the Lights

Picture this. You are in a giant convention center. There are lights on the ceiling large enough to light up an entire football stadium.

You would think that would be enough. However, on the floor, lighting is a key component of any booth. Booths don't automatically come with enough lighting.

Use it as much as possible. Lots of lights. Bright lights. Focused lights.

Put additional lighting on your logo, your headline, your product display, your tables, and your product demonstration, anything that can stand out.

Your booth will look shiny and new.

Evaluate your lighting requirements and make sure you use lots.

Use Moving Pictures

Never underestimate the use of motion to catch a person's attention. These days it is much easier to bring or rent a 60" LCD display.

Create a multimedia or animated video sequence to play in the background. Motion and video can tell your story quickly and effectively and attract prospects attention at the same time.

A three dimensional representation of a complicated engineering process can be the thing which is unique about your product and you are able to demonstrate it fast and effectively with an animated video.

I attended a conference where the presentation was a preview of the upcoming Star Wars movie displayed on a large screen with BIG sound.

It drew a big crowd every time it ran.

The only missing link was the booth staff didn't do anything with that crowd. They

used a great technique to draw the crowd
and then let them slip out of their hands by
not having a qualifying or capture plan.

*Use multimedia to draw a crowd or
demonstrate a unique product feature.*

The Famous Draw Prize

I believe that draw prizes are one of the
most misunderstood, misused, and poorly
executed show tactics out there. The logic
seems to be, "Everyone has a draw, let's
have one too."

At the same time, it can be one of the most
effective tools in your trade show
marketing inventory--when done properly.

Here are the steps:

1. Pick a draw prize.
2. Remember the fish bowl to collect
   cards.
3. Tell everyone you see to put his or
   her card in the bowl.
4. Take cards back to office.

5. Send a letter to everyone telling them about your company—include a general brochure.
6. Plan for next show.

All right, you found me out.

That's not the list at all. If you do this you are part of the crowd that isn't getting the best result from your draw prize.

If you follow that list, what you are likely to get are people who are not qualified to buy your product but who are very interested in the FREE draw prize.

And you **will** find lots of people who are after a trip to Hawaii or a Mountain Bike or a day at the spa.

The goal of the draw is to get qualified leads to identify themselves from the crowd so you can spend your valuable selling time engaging them in your sales process.

Try this approach instead.

1. Review your show goals and stay focused on your key objective.
2. Identify specifically who your target is.
3. What would make them a qualified prospect?
4. What would this prospect be interested in winning? Tie the draw into your brand or ideally give away your product or service. (if your target audience is interested in your offering it can be the best draw prize of all)
5. Make your key message and draw prize your headline. Display it prominently on your booth.
6. Train your staff to use qualifying statements or questions before just tossing the card in the booth. Don't forget to make a note on the card about what you talked about.
7. Follow up immediately with the announcement about who won the draw. Congratulate them and make a big deal about it.
8. Then commence your sales process. Call-write-call.

What you should find by using this second set of guidelines is that you will get **fewer** cards than before.

You should also get better quality in the cards because they are qualified.

And by putting a bit of effort into announcing the winner, you make yourself out to be a bit different from the other 80 draws that people may have entered into.

I attended a small local show and purposefully left my card in 46 fish bowls.

I didn't win anything but I only received THREE follow up attempts. THREE!

The point?

If you are going to use a draw prize as a strategy, plan it as an exercise in sales and for heaven's sake follow up with what you do get.

Make your use of draw prizes a marketing and selling tool.

Stay till the Closing Bell

Always keep your booth up until the
closing bell.

Almost every exhibiting agreement you
sign will have a clause in it that says you
have to be ready to display by the opening
time and you must keep your display up
until the closing time.

Human nature being what it is I would say
that about 20% or more of booths are in full
breakdown mode starting from 15 to even
30 minutes before the show is over.

It is understandable that you would want
to get the heck outta Dodge after three
days of standing, talking, dining, and
trying to keep track of your show.

You would be surprised how often the last
prospect on the floor is actually the most
interested. He or she is still there and may
be looking for some quiet time to connect
with you.

Somehow you just won't appear to be that interested when you are attempting to talk to him or her and the booth is coming down around you.

Remember the simple fact that not one of your show goals can be met by leaving the floor early. To say nothing of the impression you are leaving with other exhibitors (were they your prospects?), the event manager (keep him or her on your side) and customers on the floor.

If you watch you will see that even very large, prominent, national brand, Fortune 500 companies do this.

Don't be tempted to say, well if they do it, I can do it too.

They are dead wrong, so . . .

Keep your booth up till the closing time. Your flight doesn't leave any earlier if you are 15 minutes faster to the airport!

Pick Your Attendees Based on Show Goals

Selecting whom to bring to the show can have some of the same challenges as selecting giveaways and draw prizes.

The overall goal gets affected by the politics of the office. Many people see trade shows as a perk. Being able to travel to a foreign destination, stay in a great hotel, eat great food, and meet some new people.

When in reality trade shows are really hard work. You don't actually sleep, nor eat when you should. Many times you are frustrated things aren't going as planned and you have to stick to the script even when you are tired or would rather be doing something fun.

Simply select the best people to attend the show to best meet your show objectives.

If your show is oriented toward generating new leads, stock it with sales people. If you are doing a product launch have product management there. If you are doing a media blitz, ensure you have senior management there.

Remember the option of hiring local staff in the city you are attending.

Everyone will understand if you say your show goal is X and therefore you are bringing or hiring Y.

Minimize the politics and pick staff based on objectives.

Hold Pre-Show Training Sessions

What's the most overlooked part of show planning?

Training sessions. Tell people what your show goal is. How they will be measured.

That you have serious expectations of making the goals. That this is not a vacation.

You have a plan. You are going to stick to the plan. You expect them to follow the plan.

Setting the standard makes it easier to get compliance once the show starts and people start missing breakfast meetings or their scheduled booth duty.

Staff training should be held in the office around one week before the show.

By that time all the details will be worked out so you have answers to all the questions.

The detailed logistics are in place and can be committed to paper.

The show playbook should be complete and can be distributed. (It makes good reading on the plane.)

At that time, the show will be right around the corner so the material will not be forgotten.

Try to avoid the risk of holding a training class on the Friday afternoon before the show. There is some risk that your staff might not be able to attend. Sales reps are notorious for finding client-driven ways to miss your training session.

After all they have been selling successfully all year, what could you possibly teach them?

Lots.

Remember if you take the show seriously then others are likely to do the same.

Train, train, train.

What To Do At The Show

Make a Great First Impression

Didn't your parents always tell you that
you only have one chance for a first
impression--make it a good one?

If a delegate is going to see 50 or 100
booths, all designed by professional
display companies and professional
graphic artists, what can you do?

Get your booth designed by a professional
marketer! That's right. Let's say that you
have 50 booths to look at. Let's say that 6
are direct competition. What will make a
good first impression?

Try these differentiators.

1. Use a strong headline at the top of
your graphics. Not a logo, not a
product picture, not a list of your
technical features. Write a headline
designed to make a visitor stop and

be interested. My favourite is a killer benefit. Or a unique brand promise.

2. Brand the booth. Make a style guide so the graphics, uniform, marcom, and colors are the same.
3. Less is more. You can't do much in a 10' by 10'. Don't try. Keep it simple.
4. Keep it open. Don't cover your carpet with tables, chairs, and stuff.
5. Make the people part of the appeal. Smile. Be approachable. Be professional.

Spend some time and plan your first impression

You Are Not Running a Coffee Shop

Have you ever been in Nordstrom's or Neiman Marcus and found coffee cups on the shelves? A staff member having a sandwich at the till? The manager chewing gum?

For some reason, all of these items are commonplace on the show floor. The advice here is simple.

In the booth, do not ever eat, drink, chew gum, or leave a mess on your table.

The bigger trick is to get people to know what acceptable standards of behavior in the booth are. Put it in the show guide, mention it at the pre-show training, mention it again at the daily breakfast meeting AND remind people on the floor.

Keep Confidential Things Confidential

In the booth, don't leave confidential material on tables.

Somehow this important material grows little feet and walks away.

Ask yourself. "Who do you not want to read this?"

If they are at the show, I can almost guarantee they will read your confidential material.

Pretend You Want to Meet People

In the booth, be approachable. Stand at all times. Face the aisles. Smile at people.

Some people have this talent built in to them. You can see their energy at the show.

On 4 hours of sleep, they are go go go all day long. They love this stuff.

Others seem to be lifeless after 8 solid hours of sleep. They are not so enrolled in the show format.

If this is you—fake it! It won't kill you and it makes a different in your results.

You may surprise your own bad self by starting to see the fun in it. Less time saying, "How I hate this" and more time saying, "insert your qualifying question here"

And don't forget misery loves company so get the misery out.

Hold Please, My Phone is Ringing

Sometimes the activities I see in booths are simply amazing. You travel across the country, at great expense. You get to the booth and you keep your cell phone on— just in case.

In case of what? Remember the part about Hold Down the Fort?

Plan to be away. Make plans to leave a message that you are unable to take the call with specific instructions about call back or whom to call in the event of 'emergency'.

Not many things are as off putting to a person as trying to approach someone who is talking on the phone.

Remember, it is pretty easy to skip a booth (your booth) if you are not approachable!

Shifts are short, back up contacts are in place, and there is time to get calls later on.

Time zones can work in your favour. East coast shows can call the West coast at the end of the day. West coast shows can call the east coast first thing in the morning.

In the booth, do not take or make a cell phone call. You would not do it during an important sales call. Don't do it here.

Texting is twice as bad!

You got kids? Or a wife? Is it cool when they are texting away while you talk to them?

Why do you insist on being that guy at the trade show? Put your phone in your pocket and leave it there.

Don't take it out. Don't text. Don't worry, you'll find out where the pretty girl from booth #1104 is going to go for dinner later.

In the meantime, stay focused on the prospect you're talking to now.

Put your phone away.

You Won't Believe What Larry Did!

This idea is somewhat straightforward. On the road, things happen, great stories happen, new situations happen.

Save it.

In the booth don't talk about prospects, clients, partners, problems, issues, drunken party stories or other items you wouldn't put in your company newsletter.

If you find lots of this going on you will also find people talking to each other and not prospects. So watch for it.

Also, you are in earshot of . . . well you don't know who.

Keep your great stories till after the show hours are over and you can share them in a post show briefing or a dinner or a plane ride.

Be aware of what you say out loud. The halls have ears.

Beware of a Clique

In the booth don't talk to each other in a small group of two or more.

You are not approachable and you make it more challenging for people to come up to you.

Socialise when you return home.

Publish and Stick to a Booth Schedule

Trade shows really is one of those projects that benefits from good planning.

Spend the time in advance to figure out a schedule. Publish it, stick to it, and respect it.

This will ensure you don't have gaps in coverage and there is some parity in who covers what time.

It is best to keep your shifts short--2 hours max.

That way your sales team is not on autopilot. Remember the tip about prospecting at coffee and lunch locations?

The short shift doesn't mean that in between shifts they aren't working. It means that they get to alternate between selling in the booth and selling when sitting in the coffee area.

Give everyone his or her plan with the show playbook. Make sure you talk with them personally about what is expected and how important it will be to follow the plan once you are in the city.

Many times you will simply say, "Look, there are only three of us. We can't have a shift." That's ok too but planning 8-hour shifts for 2 people is not a plan.

There is no merit badge for superhuman feats of endurance. So try to bring enough resources to cover the booth during show hours.

And I don't need to tell you to never, ever leave the booth unattended during the show.

It really is the people that sell, not an empty booth.

This actually happens.

Plan shifts for booth duty and expect people to stick to them.

Walk the Show Floor--With a Notepad

Often at a show you will take a walk
around the floor to 'see what is going on'.

But do you walk the floor with the intent to
adjust your plan? Walk the floor and
review your competition's booth.

1. Review their messaging.
2. What has changed from last year?
3. Has their location changed? Why?
4. What is their marketing tactic?
5. What is their giveaway?
6. Watch their crowds.
7. Rank them against a checklist.

What can you learn from this?

I did a media interview and was asked.
"Should you be willing to place your booth
right beside your competition? Some
experts advise yes, others no."

My advice. If you are stronger, better,
more professional, more focused, key
messages up, booth clean, prepared, staff
trained, then the answer is absolutely, YES!

If not, then don't invite a direct comparison. But you can't make this decision if you don't have the data. And not many people can remember all the details of 6 competitive booths after a 3-day show.

Introduce Yourself to Other Exhibitors

Have you ever arrived at your booth to find a flyer or brochure from another exhibitor on your table or chairs?

If so, you may have learned that the exhibitors themselves are prospects.

While this is not a really bad thing to do, it may go against the exhibitor rules so make sure you check. Flyer drops work in part because of volume and that principle doesn't work on a target size of 100.

If the exhibitors are your targets, plan to do better.

Send them something before the show. Invite them to your booth for a special pre or post hours meeting. Offer them a special gift (make it good-relevant-valuable-not a yoyo). Walk by and introduce yourself.

Don't take up their selling time. Make sure you put your card in their draw and have them scan your badge.

You WANT to receive their mailing.

Review the scuttlebutt on the show and their experience. Maybe they are doing something well and you could adapt it.

Make contact with other exhibitors.

Respect the Time of Your Prospects

If you are talking to exhibitors and they are one of your prospects; ensure you have a coverage plan to meet them all.

Don't interfere with their selling efforts.

Let them know you just wanted to make an introduction and you will talk with them after the show.

Don't forget to ask your qualifying question so you know which is the most likely to be of interest to you afterwards.

Observe the Flow of Delegate Traffic

Event mangers often are attempting to make the exhibiting experience successful for an exhibitor at a conference.

They think about when the traffic will Come to the exhibit hall.

Where will people go after a keynote speech? Is there time at coffee to view exhibits?

You should do your own recognisance.

1. Make a note of traffic patterns and times for next year's booth placement.
2. Do they come in after lunch?
3. Do they break after a key speaker?
4. What time of day is it busiest?
5. Which day?
6. Which entrance is busiest?
7. What attractions collect people?

Write it down! Keep it in the show binder!

Borrow From Other Marketers

Walk the floor and look for GREAT marketing ideas.

What draws a crowd? Would it suit your show goals? Would it work for your business? Can you make it your own? Write them down in the show binder!

3 Places to Prospect Outside of Your Booth

Some people think that a trade show is just a trip where you give away brochures and trinkets. But the savvy salesperson knows that every opportunity to meet someone is a chance to qualify someone.

Spend time to go have coffee and lunch. Why? So you can prospect at the tables. Find out who they are. Engage them in conversation. If they are your target audience, do a card exchange. Tell them you will put them in your draw, if you have one.

Often there are shuttles to and from an event. Or like in Comdex in Las Vegas, the taxis are running back and forth day and night. Share a cab. Find out who they are. Engage them in conversation. If they are your target audience, do a card exchange. Tell them you will put them in your draw, if you have one.

Every social event you attend is a chance to prospect. The club, the restaurant, the hotel lobby. Sounds farfetched but you would be amazed at the quality connections you can make just by turning on your introduction radar.

In cities like Las Vegas 180,000 conventioneers tend to be found in the usual places and you will always be able to make a new contact.

Find out who they are. Engage them in conversation. If they are your target audience, do a card exchange. Tell them you will put them in your draw, if you have one.

See the pattern?

Never miss a chance to meet and qualify someone in the city you are in. Follow up.

Hold a Daily Breakfast Meeting

If you are on the road, meet each morning to team build and plan the day and make changes as necessary. Make it fun, tell stories, but don't make it optional.

Here is a typical agenda. (No you don't have to write it out like this-but do plan it.)

1. Review show objective
2. Tell some client stories
3. Home runs
4. Issues to address
5. Review booth schedule
6. Have a big breakfast and some fun.

Hold a daily pre show meeting.

Have a Big Breakfast

This is such a small item but I have seen it make a big difference when you don't do it.

Many generals in the battlefield know that an army with a full stomach is more effective than a hungry one.

Eat something big and heavy, pancakes, waffles, French toast, the works.

Eat something that will carry you well into the afternoon.

Things happen and you need to be able to have energy to stay with it. You also won't be tempted to go for food, eat in the booth or snarl at a prospect when your blood sugar is low.

Tell your mother I made you eat breakfast.

Review While it is Fresh in Your Mind

Meet at the end of the day, in the booth, after the close.

Immediately address any time sensitive issues. Check the results against your goals. Plan to make any necessary adjustments. Lock up your leads, cards, laptops, draws, and other irreplaceable items.

Find out if something has to be done before the next day. Are there any critical items coming up? Media interviews? Product demonstrations?

This meeting is most important at the end of the first day of a multi-day show.

Hold a daily meeting at the end of the day.

Capture Leads

These days it's not a matter of IF you will capture the leads from the show but how you will capture them. There are three primary methods.

1. **Collect Business Cards.** Collecting a business card can take the form of having them put into a draw box, exchanging them for a card of your own. Many people like to write short notes on the back of a card to refresh their memory as to the level

of interest, how qualified they are and any action items promised.

Once you have the cards in your possession, you can manually enter them into your CRM, a spreadsheet, a card scanning app for your iPhone, or use a tool like CardScan which automatically scans the cards into a database.

2. **Rent a Bar Code Scanner.** Show scanners seem like a no-brainer but this area can make a difference to your show. Some trade show scanner solutions don't work very well in the building. Have you ever seen a rep frantically trying to scan or rescan your badge while the prospect stands there patiently (or in some cases, not so patiently)?

Mostly however, they are a good idea. The cost is not too high and many shows have become quite talented at collecting delegate information at the registration desk.

Make sure you always get an electronic version of this file. It's not automatically done in all cases. It is sometimes an option. The skill-testing question is how quickly after the show do you get the file. You do want to be able to put it to work the day you return home.

Try to avoid spending too much time on the show floor doing data entry. Custom software packages that allow for data entry often put you at risk of doing the wrong thing at the wrong time. If you are behind a pedestal, head down, typing, you are not approachable and are missing opportunities to engage and qualify people.

3. **Have the delegates fill in a form.** This can take the shape of an entry form for the draw, a survey, a coupon, or an application for a prize.

The one thing to do when evaluating what way to collect the names is to stop and consider:

1. Your show goals
2. Your marketing strategy
3. Your marketing tactic
4. Your potential traffic volume
5. Number of exhibit staff
6. How much qualifying you have to do
7. What is your current lead tracking system and follow up method

By spending the time to put the data capture method in context, you will find it very easy to know whether or not you need to spend the money on scanning solutions.

But the bottom line remains the same.

Capture the leads and put them in a database.

After The Show

Can you imagine this conversation between the VP Marketing (generates leads) and the VP Sales (closes the leads)

VP M: So how were the 100 leads I sent you last month?
VP S: Great! We talked to 24 of them!
VP M: 24? What happened to the other 76?
VP S: I don't know.
VP M: You don't know? Why exactly?
VP S: We were busy selling!

You think I am crazy but that is the exact result many people experience when they return from exhibiting at a trade show.

Statistics show that fully 76% of leads are not followed up on.

What would you do with your sales department if they only followed up on one quarter of your leads? (By the way, what does a lead cost you?)

Trade show follow up is one area that can be improved simply by trying harder.

The following tips will allow you to separate yourself from your competition and other exhibitors that are competing for your prospect's attention simply by doing them.

This alone will have a huge effect on your show results.

Plan Your Post Show Follow Up Tasks

Spend some time and ensure you know what your follow up will be.

Do this **before** you go to the show.

The value in a crisp follow up plan is that you will be expecting to hop to it the moment you get back.

The more time that goes by, the more time people have to forget they talked to you (as well as 142 other people) at the show.

Think about what would be **appropriate** follow up. Some companies send a FedEx package with 5 lbs of marketing material in it. What's your budget? Could that be overkill? Will it really be effective?

Plan your follow up action plan before the show.

Call Them the First Minute you are Home

First, I should caution you not to make assumptions about what your prospects may or may not be doing when they return to their office.

The one truism today is that most people are busy. And they are even busier when they have been away from the office for a few days and return to a stack of email and phone messages.

This is even truer the higher up in an organization you go.

After the show, on day one, back in the office, call and leave a voice mail for your prospect.

Don't expect to talk to them, though.

Let them know you have their information request and will follow up as promised.

The value in this is to simply log your name into their consciousness.

Do not wait for any reason to do this.

Leave a phone message on day one back.

Send an Email or Letter

After the show and no more than 5 days after the first phone call send the promised follow up. If it is a letter, send it. If it is an email, send it.

Do not wait for any reason to do this.

Use Email Effectively

You can send three follow up emails over the next 3 weeks to politely attempt to engage your prospect in the sales cycle.

More on this later in the bonus chapter or visit www.zinmarketing.com and get the free report on email marketing strategies.

Meet With Your Sales Team Within 30 Days

Within 30 days hold a Team Review of Sales opportunities.

Discuss the quality of leads, quantity of leads, and status of the sales process. Review the sales pipeline.

Make notes in the show binder for next year's planning.

Meet With Your Sales Team Within 90 Days

Hold a meeting at Day 90 to review Sales Funnel and results.

Review Previous Show Goals and Results

When was the last time you held a quick meeting to ask the specific question? "How did we do at our last show?"

"Did we hit our targets? What went well? What was a problem? What did we learn?"

Knowing what you know now, would you return? Now that you have been to the show does the show still fit with your marketing strategy and plans?

Hold a quick meeting and do a review.

BONUS CHAPTER 1: Email Marketing Strategies

Let's just say I'm a big fan of email. Let's just say that you know that email produces the highest return of the new marketing mediums (like SEO, PPC, Social, etc) year after year after year.

Now that we agree on this important point, what's the best way to put email marketing to work for you after the show.

Before we do this I think we need to agree on what style of email marketing is going to work here. You have to pretend that you, like I do, think that email marketing is a ONE to ONE communication style.

That's hard to do when everywhere you turn, you hear the term email *blast* but keep in mind, back at the dawn of time when emails were invented they were intended to be sent from one person to another.

Personal.

That being said, the way that email is going to work the best is if you take a person-to-person approach.

Pre-Show Use of Email

Here are two specific email campaigns you can run before your next show. Give yourself *at least* 30 days to pull this off.

Often you'll be focused on your internal show prep and may not be thinking about how to maximize your attendance. Make sure you involve your customers and prospects and you'll have a better show results – no matter what goals you have in place.

If you only do one thing make sure you separate your target audience into these two groups. Don't think that a footnote at the bottom of your monthly newsletter is going to cut it.

No one sees that stuff!

Target Audience 1

Your first audience is going to be your best
customers. It could be ALL your customers
but it should be people you already do
business with you.

Why?

Because you are going to get a chance to
see them face to face and in today's
modern Internet Social world there is still
NO substitute for face-to-face meetings.

Everyone is spending time and money to
get to the same city so you should plan to
make that work to your advantage.

Since everyone's time is at a premium and
trade shows and conferences are packed
with action you'll have be to super diligent
to earn some of that time.

Key Messages

Now that you've identified that you want
to set up some meeting time with your

customers the key question is why should they meet with YOU?

You need to invent a good reason.

If you want their time you'll want to give them something, invite them to an insiders presentation, give them access to a key executive, make a special offer, announce a new product, or give them insight into your upcoming product strategies.

Whatever it is, you'll want to be laser focused on the ONE reason they should meet you.

This will be the key message of your email campaign.

Call-to-Action

Now that you have your key message you need to decide what you want them to do.

That will be the call-to-action of your email campaign.

Do you want them to randomly drop by your booth, meet with their sales rep, attend a special event, come to your hospitality suite, lunch with your CEO, or attend an exclusive insider presentation?

Whatever it is, you'll want to be laser focused on this ONE call to action.

This will be the call to action you'll use in your email campaign.

Your Email Campaign (adapt this template to your own mailing style)

1. *Will you be at the show?* Send 30 days before the show and ask if they'll be attending the show and let them know you're doing a <insert your key message here> and you'd like them to attend.
2. *We're saving a spot for you.* Send 23 days before the show and provide more details about your event. Let them know they can send a delegate in their place.
3. Now *Make Your Announcement!* Send a 2 or 3-message sequence starting at 21 days down to 10 days before the show.

You might feel like this is a lot but don't forget, they are your customers and should be fine hearing from you and there's lots going on before a show so you need to gently remind them you have something good for them.

4. *We didn't hear from you.* 7 days before the show send this message to all who didn't open any of the previous messages. Remind them of the good reasons they WANT to see you at the show. Remember the call-to-action.

5. *Last chance reminder.* Send the last business day before the show and let them know you are running out of time, space, inventory, or what ever your offer was.

There. Now you've used email in a focused and professional manner to leverage your trade show result!

Not that hard to do. Most of your competition doesn't do this. That means you are going to have a stronger show.

Don't let this wait until the last minute.

Put this email sequence in your pre-show planning checklist.

Target Audience 2

Since you've gone through the process for a single audience, start the process again with another audience.

I'd suggest you round up a list of all of your prospects and run the exact same sequence.

DO NOT USE THE SAME LANGUAGE OR COPY OR OFFER FOR YOUR PROSPECTS.

This is a different audience and you probably have a different objective!

At least you should have a different objective.

Your goal would be to move your prospects down the sales cycle closer to a close.

Leverage your show by priming the pump with email campaigns.

Post Show Use of Email

Target Audience

There are two main mistakes I see in post show use of email.

The first is the slow or late use of email. For some reason it takes too much time to get back to the office, deal with the backlog of work to catch up on, set up a mailing and get it our the door.

Time you don't have.

The best post show follow up I have seen is a sales rep sitting in their hotel room at night and sending personal emails making a connection, reminding someone of the conversation they had during the day and planting the seed that there will be a follow up conversation as soon as they both can connect.

THAT is the way you want your post show emails to sound. You want them to be their FIRST, you want them to be PERSONAL and you want them to be FREQUENT.

The second BIG mistake in post show follow up is that a general email is sent to everyone... "We met at the show..."

There's just no way that everyone you scanned is in the same situation.

The reason you separate and target your audience is so that you can send them a targeted message.

General doesn't sell. Specific sells.

Be specific with your message. Make it personal, compelling and targeted.

You will really notice a difference in results.

This big take-away here is that if your email campaigns follow this pattern you will look and feel different from your competition.

And that has to feel good!

BONUS CHAPTER 2: Social Media strategies to amplify your trade show message.

While this edition is being written social media marketing is still in its early days. By early days I mean, sure we have over a Billion users on Facebook but consistent, solid, high-ROI Facebook marketing strategies are still being road-tested.

Because of the wide range of social media strategies you COULD employ, an entire book could be written about social media marketing relative to trade shows.

You're reading this book not because you have great trade show strategies and want to layer on social, but hopefully because you want to build the foundation for profitable, high-ROI shows that will work for your business for years to come.

In that light here are three specific strategies for making your social media work WITH your trade show.

1. **Social media is an AMPLIFIER of your message.** That means you must have a message. Which in turn means your trade show goals and objectives are even more important than ever.

   Remember the conversation between Alice and the Cat in Alice's Adventures in Wonderland.

   "Would you tell me, please, which way I ought to go from here?"
   "That depends a good deal on where you want to get to," said the Cat.
   "I don't much care where--" said Alice.
   "Then it doesn't matter which way you go," said the Cat.
   "--so long as I get SOMEWHERE," Alice added as an explanation.
   "Oh, you're sure to do that," said the Cat, "if you only walk long enough."

For your social media strategy to provide leverage to your trade show you need to know your show objectives, strategies, and messages THEN you use social to support your goals.

2. **Don't let the tail wag the dog.** Step back and remember why you're using trade shows to support your business.

   Remember the effort we put into tracking and managing ROI for your shows?

   Don't let someone's fondness for the latest Social Networking strategy derail your trade show plans.

   If you're running trade shows as a key part of your marketing strategy, *make sure social supports it* and doesn't confuse you.

   For instance – if your show is based around a product announcement, then don't let your interest in LIKES derail you from getting your hottest prospects in a room to hear your announcement pitch!

Sure, Likes are important but it's not why you flew your team across the country!

Make sure you have the resources and stay focused.

Trade show marketing is flat out hard work. It takes time and details to get it right and make sure your money and opportunity aren't wasted.

If you don't have a solid social media strategy or presence in place, now is not the time to test pilot your fancy new live video aspirations.

If your social media is solid then it can play a powerful supporting role to your show or event. You get leverage that way.

But. If you're just starting to get your feet wet in social don't expect it to double your results. You're more likely to get distracted and lose focus on why you're doing shows in the first place.

Conclusion

As you can see, trade show marketing, like other forms of marketing isn't rocket science.

The most important thing you can do to get a great show result is to have a goal and a plan.

Be focused.

I have heard it said that trade show marketing is simple - but not easy.

Sometimes you have to go through the experience a few times to learn where the rough edges are and where the pitfalls are.

Each show teaches you something you can take forward to the next.

Always plan, always learn, and always get better.

Good exhibiting.

Action Items

Keep a list here of the 10 key actions you will take as a result of reading this book.

1)

2)

3)

4)

5)

6)

7)

8)

9)

10)

Refer back to them and put them in your show binder for tracking.

Notes.

The World's Greatest Trade Show Marketing Guide.
© 2014 Mitch Tarr. All Rights Reserved.

No part of this publication may be stored in a retrieval system, transmitted, or reproduced in any way without written permission by the author.

Visit www.ZinMarketing.com to register your book and get two bonus files to help with your planning.

Made in the USA
Lexington, KY
05 October 2015